SAVANNAH

⊿ GEORGIA ⊾

AND THE LOWCOUNTRY

FLORENCE MARTUS
1869 — 1943

A PHOTOGRAPHIC PORTRAIT

First published in the United States
of America by:

Twin Lights Publishers, Inc.
10 Hale Street
Rockport, Massachusetts 01966
Telephone: (978) 546-7398
http://www.twinlightspub.com

and

Yourtown Books
Telephone: (941) 262-0716

ISBN 1-885435-34-7

10 9 8 7 6 5 4 3 2 1

Book design by
SYP Design & Production, Inc.
http://www.sypdesign.com

Cover Photo by: E. B. Heston
Back Cover Photos by: James Blank,
Carrie L. Kellogg, and Rhonda Nell Fleming

Printed in China

Other titles in the Photographic Portrait series:

Cape Ann
Kittery to the Kennebunks
The Mystic Coast, Stonington to New London
The White Mountains
Boston's South Shore
Upper Cape Cod
The Rhode Island Coast
Greater Newburyport
Portsmouth and Coastal New Hampshire
Naples, Florida
Sarasota, Florida
The British Virgin Islands
Portland, Maine
Mid and Lower Cape Cod
The Berkshires
Boston
Camden, Maine
Sanibel and Captiva Islands
San Diego's North County Coast
Newport Beach, California
Phoenix and the Valley of the Sun
Wasatch Mountains, Utah
The Florida Keys
Miami and South Beach
Maryland's Eastern Shore
Asheville, North Carolina
Charleston, South Carolina

ACKNOWLEDGMENT

Twin Lights Publishers and Yourtown Books wish to thank all of the photographers who submitted their work for our consideration. Because of space limitations, we were not able to include many excellent photographs in *Savannah, Georgia and the Lowcountry: A Photographic Portrait.*

We extend our thanks to the judges whose expertise has resulted in three winning photographs, as well as a selection of photographs that describe the Savannah area beautifully. Rebecca Nolan, Professor of Photography, Savannah College of Art and Design, was raised in Twin Lakes, Wisconsin. She received a BA from the University of Wisconsin, Green Bay in Communication Processes and a M.F.A. from the University of Oregon, Eugene.

Rebecca has taught photography at the University of Kentucky, Washington University, St Louis and Webster University. Her own photography is primarily about the evidence and traces of interaction between people and the environment.

Ryan Davis Flathau is a practicing fine arts photographer who creates in a highly mannered, traditional fashion. He received his B.F.A. in photography and art education certificate from Western Michigan University. Currently he is working toward a M.F.A. in photography from Savannah College of art and Design.

Valerie Frey, Manuscript Archivist, Georgia Historical Society, whose first home was Sapelo Island, Georgia, was raised in Athens and now makes Savannah her home. She has earned both bachelors and masters degrees in art from the University of Georgia. At the Historical Society, she works to preserve historic documents and artifacts. Valerie has fifteen years of experience as a black and white photographer.

Special thanks go to the local photo and camera shops for sharing the contest information with their customers. Also to the Savannah College of Art and Design's Photography Department who most graciously hosted the judging of the contest, The Georgia Historical Society for the use of historical photographs, and The Hampton Inn, Downtown Historic District, for helping with accommodations.

We are grateful to Lauri Garbo, who wrote the captions for the photographs. She contributes regularly to various Florida Gulf Coast lifestyle magazines and newspapers. She earned a BA in English from Gustavus Adolphus College and a M. Ed from the University of South Florida. Garbo's company, "Write For You!" provides writing services for public relation firms, advertising agencies, and corporations.

Finally, our thanks to Sara Day of SYP Design & Production, Inc., who has created another beautiful book.

CONTENTS

INTRODUCTION

A deep respect for the past and a keen interest in preservation have saved the legacy of Savannah for future generations to enjoy. A survivor of wars and champion of cotton trade, Savannah's glory has withstood economic and social challenges.

Presenting a kaleidoscope of historic sites, Savannah offers a glimpse of the South's political and cultural development. An old-fashioned carriage ride through the nation's largest historical district reveals a living museum of Gothic, Victorian and plantation style architecture. A stroll in the Bonaventure Cemetery presents both natural beauty and treasured memories. The bustling River Street offers southern cuisine, whimsical boutiques, and an abundance of opportunities for people-watching. History buffs will enjoy learning more about Savannah's early military exploits with tours of Fort Pulaski and Fort McAllister. For those seeking relaxation, the beaches of Tybee Island continue to lure visitors to seaside retreats and a variety of outdoor recreational activities.

Savannah, Georgia and the Lowcountry: A Photographic Portrait is a collection of unique images captured by residents and visitors who had a desire to share their perspective with others.

Southern hospitality bursts from knowledgeable guides to friendly merchants. Savannahians present an open invitation to all visitors to explore their intriguing city and discover some personal treasures.

First Prize

FORT MCALLISTER

E. B. Heston
Hassel Blad
AGFA Velvia, F22

A lone cannon serves as a reminder of battles that were fought at Fort McAllister during the Civil War.

Since he was a youngster, E. B. Heston has been seeing his world through a camera lens. He turned his passion into a business, E. B. Enterprises that publishes postcards of Charleston and Savannah. He is a graduate of Ohio State University and is currently employed as a carriage tour guide in Charleston, South Carolina. Heston credits his award-winning photo to Dr. John Duncan, who directed him to various sites in Savannah. His photograph of Fort McAllister was accomplished after several shoots of the area. A magical combination of mist and morning light helped him capture the evocative image of history.

Second Prize

**SEAFOOD FESTIVAL ON
RIVER STREET**

Eduardo Angel
Nikon FE 2
Kodak E200

Shrimp sense their fate during the
Seafood Festival held in the Historic
District along River Street.

As a resident of Savannah, Eduardo Angel discovers a
variety of inspiring settings around every corner. His train-
ing as an architect from Los Andes University in Bogota,
Colombia, provides a unique perspective and ability to
analyze line, design, and space. These talents enrich his
study as he completes his Master of Fine Arts in
Photography at the Savannah College for Art and Design.
His photography of the Seafood Festival captures the cul-
ture and people unique to the area.

Third Prize

TYBEE ISLAND AT SUNRISE

Cathryn Shaffer
Nikon N-80
Kodak, F-11

Reflections of the morning sky are
seen in the water's rippling textures
near Tybee Island.

On a childhood walk along Savannah's then-
unpaved River Street, Cathryn Shaffer nearly
stepped on a completely flattened but per-
fect bird. That odd artwork triggered a desire
to begin sharing unique views of nature
with others. The phrase "all nature sings"
from the song *This is My Father's World*,
influenced her to begin capturing nature's
living beauty on film. Now a long-time resident of Asheville, North Carolina, Shaffer,
along with her family, operates Reign Forest
Photography. She enjoys visits with her family
at Tybee and plans far-flung travels with
camera in hand.

TUGBOAT TIES
Susan Maycock
Nikon N905
E100S

Coils of thick rope are ready to moor the tugboats when their day's work is complete.

THE RIVERFRONT

DOCKED

Susan Maycock
Nikon N905
E100S

The *Vincent Turecamo* awaits its
next assignment in the gentle
radiance of the morning sun.

WAKE-UP CALL (opposite)

Joanne Wells
Nikon
Velvia, F-22

Amidst the lavender glow of dawn,
the towers on the Westin Hotel
serve as a mighty landmark along
River Street.

WORKING THE WATERWAYS

Diane L. Strickland

The fully loaded ocean carrier creeps past the historic Riverfront district.

PORT OF SAVANNAH *(opposite)*

Diane L. Strickland

Unloading at the docks requires both cranes and crew. A cylinder of steel coil descends slowly from above.

SAGA CREST

Lila Kirkwood
Minolta X700
Fuji Velvia, F-11

Savannah's seaport was the first in Georgia's history. Today it is one of the busiest seaports in the United States.

SOUTHERN BRIDGEWORK *(opposite)*

Lila Kirkwood
Minolta X700
Fuji Velvia, F-22

An engineering feat known as the Talmadge Bridge looms above the river and directs Highway 17 to South Carolina.

SAVANNAH RIVER

E. B. Heston
Hassel Blad
AGFA Velvia, F22

A wooden vessel in the foreground
contrasts with the modern bridge
and mammoth cargo ships along
the Savannah River.

TUG ESCORT

Diane L. Strickland

Perky tugboats flank either side of the cargo ship as it passes through the Port of Savannah.

IN THE ROW

Eduardo Angel
Nikon FE 2
Kodak E200

Seafood enthusiasts enjoy fresh oysters at Savannah's Seafood Festival.

SEAGULL RESTING *(opposite)*

Diane L. Strickland

An inquisitive seagull surveys the flow of traffic in the seaport.

THE BRIDGE AT NIGHT (top)

Eduardo Angel
Nikon FE 2
Kodak E200

A geometric glow highlights the
Talmadge Bridge at night. Moored
yachts add to the luminescence of
festive lighting.

HEADING OUT (bottom)

Susan Maycock
Nikon N905
E100S

Predawn preparations begin along
the seaport as seasoned captains
anticipate another challenging day
on the water.

ST. PATRICK'S DAY ON THE RIVERFRONT

Hunter Photography

Savannah's biggest annual bash. Thousands come every year to celebrate St. Patrick's Day.

RIVER STREET AT CHRISTMAS

Diane L. Strickland

An old-fashioned ice cream parlor, complete with rootbeer floats and frothy malts, beckons shoppers along River Street.

FACTOR'S WALK *(opposite)*

Lila Kirkwood
Minolta X700
Fuji Velvia, F-8

Located between River Street and Bay Street, Factor's Walk welcomes shoppers and those who are intrigued with the historical Riverfront site.

DOWNTOWN SAVANNAH (top)

Carol Gordon
Nikon N6006
Kodak

The golden dome of City Hall maintains its stately dominance over the Riverfront. Patriotic paddlewheels await a throng of tourists.

GEORGIA QUEEN RIVERBOAT (bottom)

Charles E. Reist
Kodak VR35
Fuji 200

The Georgia Queen Riverboat provides numerous sightseeing tours and a nautical form of entertainment. A view of Savannah from the river offers an interesting perspective.

THE WAVING GIRL (opposite)

Carol Gordon
Nikon N6006
Kodak

Located at the east entrance to River Street, the sculpture of Savannah's Waving Girl references Florence Martus who waved a white handkerchief to sailors as they passed to and from Savannah.

FLORENCE MARTUS
1869 — 1943
SAVANNAH'S WAVING GIRL

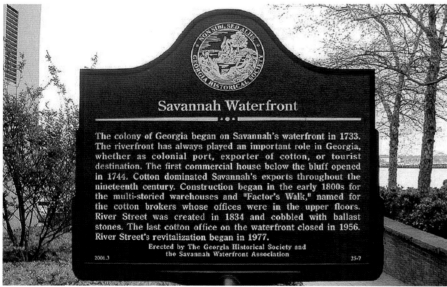

STONE STEPS TO FACTOR'S WALK *(above)*

Curt Avery
Minolta 400
Kodak 800

Climbing the stone steps from River Walk to Factor's Walk provides an authentic glimpse into the district's architectural past.

WATERFRONT HIGHLIGHTS *(left)*

Deanna L. Predmore
Nikon Coolpix 950
Digital

Savannah's rich history is documented throughout the city with informative plaques outlining highlights of the most prominent landmarks.

LAWTON FAMILY GRAVESITES *(opposite)*

Cathryn Shaffer
Nikon N-80
Kodak, F-8

In addition to serving in the Civil War, General Lawton served the Georgia legislature and railroad board. His arched memorial in the distance is surrounded by family members' gravesites.

RIVER STREET

Deanna L. Predmore
Nikon Coolpix 950
Digital

Cobblestone roads and railroad tracks serve as reminders of River Street's origin in 1834. Now lined with eclectic shops and restaurants, the renovated waterfront warehouse welcomes diners, shoppers and festival attendees.

RIVERFRONT *(opposite)*

Paul Nurnberg

Patches of green beyond the riverfront outline the twenty-one squares that were incorporated into the city's design in 1733 by General James Oglethorpe. In the foreground, River Street warehouses that were once a mecca for trade have been refurbished and now beckon diners and shoppers.

MYSTERIES OF MERCER

E. B. Heston
Hassel Blad
AGFA Velvia, F22

Shuttered windows and shadowed doorways of the Mercer House protect the secrets of Jim Williams and Danny Hansford who both lived and died at this location.

HISTORIC DOWNTOWN

FLOWING FOUNTAIN

E. B. Heston
Hassel Blad
AGFA Velvia, F22

Mythological creatures and Greek
figures adorn the elaborate cast iron
fountain commissioned for the cen-
ter of Forsyth Park in 1858.

HISTORIC HOUSE *(opposite)*

James Blank
Pentax 67
Ektachrome 64, F-16

Located on the southern edge of
Monterey Square, the Mills Bee Lane
house, a red brick Georgian Revival
house, was completed in 1910.

CHARMING ABODE

James Blank
Pentax 67
Ektachrome 64, F-16

Throughout Savannah's Historic District numerous examples of plantation style architecture has been preserved. Shaded verandahs and tall windows maximize the cooling effects of gentle summer breezes.

**MONUMENT AT MADISON
SQUARE**

E. B. Heston
Hassel Blad
AGFA Velvia, F22

A statue of the courageous Sergeant
William Jasper immortalizes his
determination to uphold his regi-
ment during the Siege of Savannah.

SPRING

Joanne Wells
Nikon
Velvia, F-22

The stone monuments of man contrast greatly with the natural beauty of nature in the Bonaventure Cemetery.

TEMPLE MICKUE ISRAEL *(opposite)*

E. B. Heston
Hassel Blad
AGFA Velvia, F22

The only Gothic synagogue in America, the Mickue Israel Temple, was built in 1878 and is located in the Historic District. The original Torah brought by the English founders of Savannah in 1733 is on display in the temple.

COLONIAL DAMES HOUSE

James Blank
Pentax 67
Ektachrome 64, F-11

Prominent architect John Norris designed a fitting tribute to Savannah's rich history, the Colonial Dames House on the west side of Lafayette Square.

DOLPHIN DOWNSPOUT *(left)*

E. B. Heston
Hassel Blad
AGFA Velvia, F8

Inventive and classic architectural elements are found throughout Savannah. This downspout highlights Savannah's significant relationship with the sea.

DOUBLE HOUSE

James Blank
Pentax 67
Ektachrome 64, F-11

Warehouses, factories and tene-
ments have been transformed into
quaint inns and luxurious residences
in the preserved areas of Savannah.

SITTING PRETTY

James Blank
Pentax 67
Ektachrome 64, F-11

Taking advantage of a corner site,
this Victorian home sets the tone for
the entire row of historic architectural delights.

VICTORIAN HOMES *(opposite)*

James Blank
Pentax 67
Ektachrome 64, F-11

A row of Victorian homes decked
with intricate trim detail and cool,
shaded verandahs are reminiscent of
a genteel era. Over 2,350 architectural
and historically significant buildings
are located in the 2.5 square mile
Historic District.

MAGNOLIA

Joanne Wells
Nikon
Velvia, F-22

A symbol of the genteel South, the magnolia bursts forth fragrant blossoms in the spring. This close-up view reveals the unfathomable details of nature.

THE GOLDEN DOME *(opposite)*

Lila Kirkwood
Minolta X700
Fuji Velvia, F-11

The brilliant golden dome of City Hall rises above the trees on the site of the Old City Exchange.

PEACE AND TRANQUILLITY

Melissa M. Fraser
Cannon EOS Elan 11E
Kodak Gold 200, F-11

The splendor of gild, dramatic arches, and religious murals create an inspiring place of worship at the Cathedral of St. John the Baptist.

CATHEDRAL OF ST. JOHN THE BAPTIST (opposite)

James Blank
Pentax 67
Ektachrome 64, F-11

Gilded spires, painted arches and French Gothic ornamental work characterize the Cathedral of St. John the Baptist on Harris Street. Serving as the seat of the Diocese of Savannah, the church was founded in 1799.

THE KEHOE HOUSE

James Blank
Pentax 67
Ektachrome 64, F-16

Stone balustrades, capitals, and corbels add the appropriate accents to this Italian-style villa.

LINED UP (*opposite*)

James Blank
Pentax 67
Ektachrome 64, F-16

A small group of leading citizens rallied and incorporated the Historic Savannah Foundation to save many homes including handsome 19th century row houses.

IRONWORK

James Blank
Pentax 67
Ektachrome 64, F-16

Elaborate ironwork detail and seasonal blooms enhance the otherwise stark "doublehouse" along Monterey Square.

HEAVY METAL (opposite)

James Blank
Pentax 67
Ektachrome 64, F-16

Shadowed silhouettes of iron slats fall upon the stone walls of a home in the Historic District.

TELFAIR FAMILY MANSION

James Blank
Pentax 67
Ektachrome 64, F-11

Deemed the oldest art museum in the South, the Telfair Family Mansion now houses a permanent art collection as well as authentic period rooms.

TRADITION

James Blank
Pentax 67
Ektachrome 64, F-16

Built in the late 1800's, this four-story Italiante home is an example of the traditional Savannah style.

FLOWING GREEN (opposite)

Joanne Wells
Nikon
Velvia, F-22

Savannah is famous for its St. Patrick's Day celebrations. Green water flowing from the fountain in Forsyth Park is just one of the unusual green sites found around the city on this popular holiday.

SHAKESPEARE IN THE PARK *(above)*

Eduardo Angel
Nikon FE 2
Kodak E200

Outdoor events abound in
Savannah's numerous parks and
outdoor facilities. Shakespeare fans
enjoy the Bard's work even more
when performed outdoors.

HISTORIC DOWNTOWN *(left)*

Hunter Photography

Savannah was the first city in North
America that was planned on a sys-
tem of squares. Oglethorpe's sym-
metrically designed grid included
strategically placed parks throughout
the city. In the foreground Forsyth
Park provides a beautiful haven for
city dwellers.

CITY HALL

Eduardo Angel
Nikon FE 2
Kodak E200

As the clock approaches midnight, the emerald gleam from the dome of City Hall casts its spell on the adjacent streets.

HEAVEN ON EARTH

Carrie L. Kellogg
Canon Elan 7
Kodak 100

Throughout the burial grounds, elaborate sculptures, tombstones and inscriptions create a fascinating tour of old Savannah society.

ST. PAUL'S GREEK ORTHODOX CHURCH

Ryan Smith
Cambo 4x5
Kodak E100S

Classic architectural elements including
stately columns and capitals uphold the
pediment of St. Paul's Greek Orthodox
Church in downtown Savannah.

GRACIE

Carrie L. Kellogg
Canon Elan 7
Kodak 100

A mirror of the past, Gracie seems to look beyond the natural beauty of Bonaventure Cemetery to an even more serene destiny.

CARRIAGE RIDE *(opposite)*

James Blank
Pentax 67
Ektachrome 64, F-11

Old-fashioned carriages clip-clop throughout the Historic District, enhancing the journey back in time. The historically significant Independent Presbyterian Church showcases a combination of wood and stone architecture.

MOURNING MERCER *(above)*

Diane L. Strickland

Famous song titles including, "Accentuate the Positive," were created by lyricist, composer and singer Johnny Mercer. He was born in Savannah, Georgia in 1909 and his grave is located in Bonaventure Cemetery.

REMEMBRANCE *(left)*

Diane L. Strickland

The serenity and beauty of Bonaventure Cemetery is comparable to its rich history. Hundreds of live oaks surround the grounds that host gravesites of famous Georgia citizens.

ARCHANGEL MEMORIAL *(opposite)*

Kandie K. Strefling
Nikon
Kodak, 16

Aged and broken, the sculpted angel continues to grasp fresh bouquets in remembrance of loved ones who have left this world.

DELIGHTFUL DISPLAY
Mark D. Forehand
Minolta 202
Fujichrome, F-8-5.6

Rich in bloom, Savannah's spring-time display of azaleas and flowering dogwoods enrich the beauty of Bonaventure Cemetery.

ANGEL HOLDING SHELL

Diane L. Strickland

The angelic alabaster profile is one of many inspirational sculptures found in Bonaventure Cemetery.

TOWNHOUSE ROW *(opposite)*

Karin M. Smith
Nikon F100
Ektachrome 200

Prestigious townhouse addresses offer prime locations, historical value and gracious living among some of Savannah's squares and neighborhoods.

RAIL STATION *(top)*

Eduardo Angel
Nikon FE 2
Kodak E200

Visitors take a break amidst the glorious history of the Central Georgia Railroad. The exhibition hall displays Savannah's cherished memorabilia.

GRILLIN' *(bottom)*

Eduardo Angel
Nikon FE 2
Kodak E200

Morning light filters through the smoke rising from the barbecue grills at Forsyth Park. A savory picnic will be ready for the lunch crowd.

MULBERRY INN LOBBY *(opposite)*

Ryan Smith
Cambo 4x5
Kodak EPY

The English grandfather clock reminds guests of the hour in the lobby of the Mulberry Inn. Having served as a livery, stable, and cotton warehouse, the multifunctional site now basks in the luxury of affluence.

ESCAPING LIGHT *(above)*

James Everett Masterson
Canon AE-1 Program
Fuji Super HQ, 100 ASA, F8

Metal studs rise and begin to alter Savannah's evolving skyline. Glowing beyond, the illuminated dome of City Hall upholds the city's historic stature.

MONUMENT TO THE CONFEDERACY *(right)*

Ron Gordon
Minolta 7000 Maxuum
Kodak

Emerging from an imaginary sea, classic figures blast a cool invitation to passersby in Forsyth Park.

BLUE LIGHT WHITE LIGHT *(opposite)*

James Everett Masterson
Canon AE-1 Program
Fuji Super HQ, 100 ASA, F8

Local eateries bustle with the onset of evening, while the city beyond unwinds from the events of the day.

HOME SWEET HOME *(top)*

Melissa M. Fraser
Cannon EOS Elan 11E
Kodak Gold 200, F-11

Creeping ivy will soon encompass the façade of this charming old Savannah home. Antique fashioned lace curtains, tall windows and intricate ironwork combine to create dramatic curb appeal.

EIGHT STEPS HOME *(bottom)*

Melissa M. Fraser
Cannon EOS Elan 11E
Kodak Gold 200, F-11

Three distinct versions of iron railings define the identical row of residences along this brick-lined walk.

THE CHEROKEE ROSE

Rhonda Nell Fleming
N-60 Nikon
Kodak GC 400

As the state flower, the annual blossoming of the Cherokee Rose reminds Georgians of their heritage. The five-petalled, white flowers climb up stone walls and trellises in many Savannah gardens.

WEST SIDE

James Everett Masterson
Canon AE-1 Program
Fuji Super HQ, 100 ASA, F8

Dimly lit, the "westside" takes on
an air of mystery and romance.

THE GLOBE *(opposite)*

Benjamin Freshman
Minolta Maxxum
Ektachrome, F-11

A surreal image appears on
DeRenne Avenue when the "globe"
is illuminated. An unused natural
gas storage tank, the globe mural
has become an interesting landmark.

CLOSE-UP TO THE MERCER MANSION

Rhonda Nell Fleming
N-60 Nikon
Kodak GC 400

A collage of natural elements—brick, stone, wood and foliage merge to create an artistic view and shroud the mysteries of the Mercer Mansion.

GOOD AND EVIL *(opposite)*

Rhonda Nell Fleming
N-60 Nikon
Kodak GC 400

In John Berendt's best-seller, *Midnight in the Garden of Good and Evil*, the Mercer House on Monterey Square allows a glimpse into the scandals and lifestyle of the popular protagonist Jim Williams.

ANGEL IN BONAVENTURE

Carrie L. Kellogg
Canon Elan 7
Kodak 100

The gentle touch of God's angel and scripture passage, "Blessed are the pure of heart for they shall see God," reassures family and friends of eternal life in heaven.

COLONIAL PARK CEMETERY (*opposite*)

Carol Gordon
Nikon N6006
Kodak

The contrasting feelings that surround death are reflected in the sadness of the weeping willow and the new life springing forth from the colorful blossoms.

A BETTER PLACE

Carrie L. Kellogg
Canon Elan 7
Kodak 100

The live oaks festooned with Spanish moss seem to reflect the sagging spirits of those in mourning. The stone monument that portrays a thoughtful young woman is one of many artistic interpretations in Bonaventure Cemetery.

CRAPE MYRTLE TREES

Charles E. Reist
Pentax IQZoom 80-E
Fuji 400

Springtime blooms of the crape
myrtle create a colorful promenade
for the residents along this compact
line of row houses.

IRON SUNFLOWER

Mary Elizabeth May
Minolta Zoom 90

Animated sunflower faces guard the
entrance to a passage that leads to a
private, sunlit courtyard.

WINDING WELCOME

Charles E. Reist
Pentax IQZoom 80-E
Fuji 400

A decorative curved iron railing creates
a dramatic entrance to a renovated
townhouse steeped in history.

CHRISTMAS COLOR

Diane L. Strickland

Seasonal poinsettia blooms adorn
the entrances to many of Savannah's
historic inns on Oglethorpe Street.

TIMOTHY BONTICOU HOUSE

Joanne Wells
Nikon
Velvia, F-22

Rustic charm of hand-hewn wood
distinguishes the Timothy Bonticou
House from others in the Historic
District.

COTTON EXCHANGE (opposite)

Rhonda Nell Fleming
N-60 Nikon
Kodak GC 400

When cotton was king, the Savannah
Cotton Exchange was filled with bro-
kers trading "white gold" for riches
that made the city prosper.

THE FOUNDER

Carrie L. Kellogg
Canon Elan 7
Kodak 100

The stately English General James
Edward Oglethorpe oversees the 13th
colony of the New World. Oglethorpe founded Savannah in 1733.

MONUMENTAL

Karin M. Smith
Nikon F100
Ektachrome 200, F16

Built nearly a century ago, City Hall
at the north end of Bull Street aligns
itself perfectly on Oglethorpe's sym-
metrical city grid.

CELESTIAL (opposite)

Rhonda Nell Fleming
N-60 Nikon
Kodak GC 400

Spires cast in patina on Wesley
Monumental Methodist Church on
Calhoun Square are reminders of the
colonists' search for religious free-
dom in the New World.

THE GINGERBREAD HOUSE
Carrie L. Kellogg
Canon Elan 7
Kodak 100

Unusual colors and trim create
a storybook setting that is both
intriguing and enchanting.

SPRING AT FORSYTH PARK *(above)*

Carrie L. Kellogg
Canon Elan 7
Kodak 100

Named for Governor John Forsyth, Forsyth Park was designed in 1851 and its original design created by Bavarian landscape gardener William Bischoff. The fountain is based on a similar design that was exhibited in London in 1851.

HAMILTON TURNER HOUSE

Carrie L. Kellogg
Canon Elan 7
Kodak 100

Dating from 1873, this Second Empire style mansion was owned by Mandy Hillis until 1997 when new owners transformed it into a bed and breakfast.

GARDEN GLIMPSE

Rhonda Nell Fleming
N-60 Nikon
Kodak GC 400

Beyond the arched iron gate and
wooden doors, a private garden is
revealed. A stone fountain and brick
pathway entice passersby to pause
and perhaps stroll.

COLONIAL PARK CEMETERY

Carrie L. Kellogg
Canon Elan 7
Kodak 100

Strolling and reading old tombstone
inscriptions can shed light on
Savannah's past. The cemetery is the
final resting-place for Savannahians
who died between 1750 and 1853.

THE CHESTNUT HOUSE

Carrie L. Kellogg
Canon Elan 7
Kodak 100

Built in 1897 for Joseph Chestnut, a naval stores factor and dealer, the two-story Queen Anne style house with twin copper-roofed turret porches is located at the southern end of Forsyth Park.

DOGWOOD BLOSSOM *(opposite)*

Rhonda Nell Fleming
N-60 Nikon
Kodak GC 400

Symbolic of the sweetness of the South, dogwood blossoms offer the fragrant springtime promise of another miraculous rebirth.

SEEING REDFORD

Rhonda Nell Fleming
N-60 Nikon
Kodak GC 400

Savannah's historic backdrop serves as the setting for many of Hollywood's productions. Crews focus their attention on Robert Redford during the filming of *Bagger Vance*.

**FIRE STATION
CIRCA 1941**

Courtesy of the Georgia Historical
Society, Savannah, Georgia

Savannah was on the cutting edge
with inventions like the cotton gin
and in 1911 with the first motorized
fire department in the United States.
This photograph taken in 1941
depicts a prepared and proud fire-
fighting team.

**BOY ON BICYCLE
CIRCA 1930** *(opposite)*

Courtesy of the Georgia Historical
Society, Savannah, Georgia

Couriers pedaled their way throughout Savannah's streets in the 1930's.
The Lucas Theater in the background
was originally built in 1921 and
recently reopened after a 13-year
period of restoration.

**SOLMS HOTEL ON TYBEE ISLAND
CIRCA 1932**

Courtesy of the Georgia Historical
Society, Savannah, Georgia

Wealthy patrons of the Solms Hotel
gather for afternoon tea and enjoy
the parade of people and Model-T's
along the beach.

**MEDDIN BROTHERS MEAT
MARKET CIRCA 1930'S**

Courtesy of the Georgia Historical
Society, Savannah, Georgia

A slaughter house and retail outlet,
Meddin Brothers Meat Market provided poultry, beef and pork for local
consumers.

BUG

Sandra Mudge
Canon
Fuji 400

Haircut prices may have changed
over the years, but the cash register
at Beaver's Barbershop continues to
ring up sales for local patrons.

BEAVER'S BARBERSHOP

Sandra Mudge
Canon
Fuji 400

Beaver's Barbershop, the oldest barbershop in Savannah, houses func-
tional remnants of the past like this
worn display cabinet.

LAUNDRY DAY

LaMoille Dopson
Nikon F2
Kodak SW Transparency, F 5.6

Mr. Futch greets customers at his patriotically painted launderette. Family businesses that span the generations are an interesting part of Savannah's history.

FRIENDS PLAYING CHECKERS

LaMoille Dopson
Nikon F2
Kodak 100, F-8

Old-fashioned past times like a
friendly game of checkers unite both
young and old during a chilly morning match.

SAVANNAH'S CITY MARKET

Melissa M. Fraser
Cannon EOS Elan 11E
Kodak Gold 200, F-8

Created for strolling pedestrian traffic, City Market provides abundant window shopping, intimate gallery settings, as well as unique restaurants.

FEEDING TIME

Karin M. Smith
Nikon F100
Ektachrome 200, F8

A nostalgic carriage ride offers one of the most relaxing ways to tour the Historic District and soak up the charm of Savannah's past.

WALL ART

Mary Elizabeth May
Pentax K-1000
Kodak Royal 100

An outdoor installation of the artist Partick Dougherty hangs on the wall of Habesham Hall, Savannah College of Art and Design.

INVITING PLACE TO SIT

Carol Gordon
Nikon N6006
Kodak

At the Six Pence Pub the influence of England and King George still flourish. The British telephone booth and pub front recreate the historical era.

SKIDAWAY SUNRISE

Carol Verneuil
Canon Elan
Velvia, F-22

An inland island surrounded by marsh
and other wetlands, Skidaway Island
offers both historic and natural beauty
as seen in this inspiring sunrise.

TYBEE

ISLAND AND THE COAST

SUNSET BEACH FENCE

Megan Senior
Nikon N70

The sun sets along the five miles of
unspoiled beaches on Tybee Island.

TYBEE PIER AT SUNRISE

Joanne Wells
Nikon
Velvia, F-22

The glowing ball of the rising sun emerges from the calm horizon, creating a silhouette of Tybee Pier and enthusiastic fishermen.

JEKYLL ISLAND.

Bill Mattern
Nikon FE
Kodachrome G4

Foam from an active surf builds on
the shoreline of Jekyll Island. In the
early 19th century, the island served
as an exclusive retreat for the wealth-
iest and most exclusive guests from
around the world.

WINTER AT TYBEE ISLAND

Diane L. Strickland

A young girl interrupts seagulls searching for breakfast on a brisk morning run along the shore.

KEEPING WATCH *(top)*

Charles E. Reist
Pentax IQZoom 80-E
Fuji 400

Near the pier and pavilion, a duo of lifeguards monitor the beach and swimming area along Tybee's shore.

WAVES ON THE JETTY *(bottom)*

Elaine J. Oehmich
Nikkormat FT
400, F-22

Inspired by the salty Atlantic Ocean, the Yamacrow Indians appropriately named the island *Tybee*, meaning *salt*.

ON THE BLUFF

Diane L. Strickland

Sheltered by the shade of a live oak, a decorated Christmas tree greets visitors approaching this coastal cottage on the Isle of Hope.

BEACH COTTAGES AND TYBEE LIGHTHOUSE

Diane L. Strickland

Modern beach cottages block the view of Tybee Lighthouse, Georgia's oldest and tallest lighthouse, dating back to 1773.

BRANCHES

Elaine J. Oehmich
Nikkormat FT
400, F-11

The Atlantic from the shores of Little
Tybee as seen through fallen trees.
Bare weathered branches provide
contrast to the smooth, calm
Atlantic waters in the distance.

PREDAWN AT TYBEE ISLAND

Susan Maycock
Nikon N905
E100S

Soft hues of lavender, rose and blue
intermingle in the calm predawn on
the coast of Tybee Island.

PIER AT NIGHT (opposite)

Kandie K. Strefling
Nikon
Kodak, 5.6

Calm water and a low tide create a
serene atmosphere for beachcombers
on an evening stroll down the pier.

TYBEE ISLAND MUSEUM

James Blank
Pentax 67
Ektachrome 64, F-16

Located in one of Fort Screven's batteries, the Tybee Island Museum houses a collection that follows Tybee from the arrival of the Euchee Indians to World War II.

GREAT BLUE HERON

Rhonda Nell Fleming
N-60 Nikon
Kodak GC 400

An alert and determined blue heron scouts for seafood delicacies in the lagoon on Skidaway Island.

**ROAD TO BETHESDA HOME
FOR BOYS**

Carol Verneuil
Canon Elan
Velvia, F-22

Morning fog still lingers along the
canopied road leading to Bethesa
Home for Boys, America's oldest
existing children's home.

VIEW FROM BETHESDA HOME FOR BOYS

Carol Verneuil
Canon Elan
Velvia, F-22

Nestled on 650 acres along the Moon River, the grounds surrounding Bethesda offer a tranquil retreat for thoughtful mediation.

THE LIGHTHOUSE ON TYBEE ISLAND

Charles E. Reist
Pentax IQZoom 80-E
Fuji 400

Ominous clouds approach the Tybee Lighthouse, America's third-oldest lighthouse that stands 154 feet tall.

IT TICKLES MY TOES

Carol Gordon
Nikon N6006
Kodak

The refreshing Atlantic Ocean waters swirl around a toddler's toes and ankles.

**THE MURAL AT TYBEE
PIER PAVILION**

Charles E. Reist
Pentax IQZoom 80-E
Fuji 400

A colorful underwater scene highlights area sea life that exists near
the coast of Tybee Island, which
consists of five square miles.

© Paul Nurnberg 2001

TYBEE LIGHTHOUSE *(opposite)*

Paul Nurnberg

Soaring 145 feet up, the Tybee Lighthouse is an historical landmark. Located across from Fort Screven, the lighthouse is the oldest and tallest in Georgia. Guests are invited to climb 178 steps to the observation deck for a magnificent view of the surrounding area.

TYBEE ISLAND

Hunter Photography

Located just 14 miles east of Savannah, Tybee Island, a small barrier island, offers a retreat for Savannahians and a destination for beach-bound visitors. Museums, monuments, and historic sites located on the island highlight the island's contribution to the development of the area.

FIRE POWER

James Blank
Pentax 67
Ektachrome 64, F-22

Fort Pulaski's artillery was no match
for the Union's new experimental
rifled cannon, which rendered the
fort indefensible.

**FORT PULASKI NATIONAL
MONUMENT** *(opposite)*

James Blank
Pentax 67
Ektachrome 64, F-22

Eighteen years of intermittent con-
struction was needed to create this
massive two-tiered structure in the
shape of a fractured hexagon.

ARCHES *(above)*
James Blank
Pentax 67
Ektachrome 64, F-16

Twenty-five million bricks and 70-foot pilings driven into the mud support Fort Pulaski, which was named after Count Casimir Pulaski, a Polish soldier patriot who died in his effort to save Savannah during the Civil War.

BUNKING IT *(left)*
Mary Elizabeth May
Minolta Zoom 90

Confederate soldiers quarters provided for the basic essentials. Built in 1847 to protect the nation's shorelines from attack, Fort Pulaski was ultimately utilized during the Civil War.

STEPS OF THE PAST

Carrie L. Kellogg
Canon Elan 7
Kodak 100

Stronger than Savannah gray brick, red brick imported from Maryland and Virginia are used to fortify upper walls and arches. The new rifled cannon used in 1862 rendered brick forts obsolete.

FORT PULASKI NATIONAL MONUMENT

Hunter Photography

Built on Cockspur Island between 1829 and 1847, Fort Pulaski fell during the Civil War on its second day of bombardment. The fort has been restored and is now operated by the National Park Service.

FORT PULASKI *(opposite)*

Mary Ann May
Minolta X700
AGFA Optima 125

Enslaved African Americans, who provided much of the labor involved in building the fort, were responsible for building this series of red brick arches that create a clandestine environment.

CONTRIBUTORS

Eduardo Angel
1910 Skidaway Road
Savannah, GA 31404
7, 20, 22, 56, 57, 68(2)

Curt Avery
24 Barrington Circle
Savannah, GA 31409
28

James Blank
1110 Red Maple Drive
Chula Vista, CA 91910
*back cover, 35, 36, 40, 41, 42,
43, 47, 48, 49, 50, 51, 52–53,
54, 61, 114, 122, 123, 124*

LaMoille Dopson
104-B W. Broughton Street
Savannah, GA 31401
98, 99

Rhonda Nell Fleming
315 E. 51st Street
Savannah, GA 31405
*back cover, 72–73, 76, 77, 83, 85, 88,
90, 91, 115*

Mark D. Forehand
212 Bonaventure Road
Thunderbolt, GA 31405
64–65

Melissa M. Fraser
1536 Inland Avenue, Apt. C
Charleston, SC 29412
46, 72(2), 100

Benjamin Freshman
205 E. Park Avenue
Savannah, GA 31401
74

Carol Gordon
530 Oak Bay Drive
Osprey, FL 34229
1, 26, 27, 78, 101, 118

Ron Gordon
530 Oak Bay Drive
Osprey, FL 34229
71

E. B. Heston
P.O. Box 558
Ravenel, SC 29470
cover, 4–5, 18, 32–33, 34, 37, 39, 40

Carrie L. Kellogg
1502 Noble Oaks Drive
Savannah, GA 31406
*back cover, 58, 60, 79(2), 84,
86, 87(2), 88, 89, 125*

Lila Kirkwood
13 Stoneledge Drive
Portland, ME 04102
16, 17, 25, 45

James Everett Masterson
312 ¹/₂ W. Taylor
Savannah, GA 31401
70, 71, 74

Bill Mattern
429 Country Way
Scituate, MA 02066
106

Mary Anne May
193 Lakecrest Drive N.E.
Milledgeville, GA 31061
127

Mary Elizabeth May
25 A Little Knob Road
Asheville, NC 28803
81, 101, 124

Susan Maycock
908 Standiford Drive
Malvern, PA 19355
10–11, 12, 22, 112

Sandra Mudge
146 Spinnaker Walk
Savannah, GA 31410
96, 97

Elaine J. Oehmich
197 Oak Street #7
Boone, NC 28607
108, 111

Deanna L. Predmore
306 Coronation Drive
Amherst, NY 14226
28, 30

Charles E. Reist
1613 Livingstone Street
Sarasota, FL 34231
26, 80, 81, 108, 118, 119

Megan Senior
413 A East Gaston Street
Savannah, GA 31401
104

Cathryn Shaffer
1796 Hendersonville Road
Asheville, NC 28803
8–9, 29

Karin M. Smith
1630 Highland Farm Drive
Suwanee, GA 30024
67, 84, 100

Ryan Smith
836 Maupas Avenue
Savannah, GA 31401
58–59, 69

Kandie K. Strefling
1524 E. 53rd Street
Savannah, GA 31404
63, 113

Diane L. Strickland
38 Passaic Court
Richmond Hill, GA 31324
*14, 15, 18–19, 21, 24, 62(2),
66, 82, 107, 109, 110*

Carol Verneuil
33 Woody Lane
Westport, CT 06880
3, 102–103, 116, 117

Joanne Wells
114 Herb River Drive
Savannah, GA 31406
13, 38, 44, 55, 82, 105